MW01109813

IMPACT MY LIFE

Biblical Mentoring Simplifed

• Study Guide •

Elisa Pulliam
moretobe.com

© Copyright 2013 by Elisa Pulliam. All Rights Reserved.

The right of Elisa Pulliam to be identified as author and copyright owner of this work is asserted by Elisa Pulliam.

Unless otherwise indicated, all Scripture quotations are taken from the Holy Bible, New Living Translation, copyright © 1996, 2004, 2007 by Tyndale House Foundation. Used by permission of Tyndale House Publishers, Inc., Carol Stream, Illinois 60188. All rights reserved.

Scripture quotations marked ESV are from The Holy Bible, English Standard Version® (ESV®), copyright © 2001 by Crossway, a publishing ministry of Good News Publishers. Used by permission. All rights reserved.

Scripture quotations marked MSG are from THE MESSAGE. Copyright © by Eugene H. Peterson 1993, 1994, 1995, 1996, 2000, 2001, 2002. Used by permission of NavPress Publishing Group.

This work is licensed under the Creative Commons Attribution-NonCommercial-NoDerivs 3.0 Unported License. To view a copy of this license, visit http://creativecommons.org/licenses/by-nc-nd/3.0/ or send a letter to Creative Commons, 171 Second Street, Suite 300, San Francisco, California, 94105, USA.

All rights reserved. No part of this publication may be reproduced or transmitted, in any form by any means without the prior written permission of the author, nor be otherwise circulated in any form of binding or cover, other than that in which it is published and without a similar condition being imposed on the subsequent purchaser.

The purchaser of this publication indemnifies Elisa Pulliam and her companies, MoretoBe.com, ElisaPulliam.com, and Authentic Life Inc., and the directors, officers, employees and agents of those companies, from and against all losses, claims, damages and liabilities which arise out of any use of this publication and/or any application of its content.

Please understand that there are some links contained in this book that I may benefit from financially. The material in this book may include information, products or services by third parties. Third party materials contain the products and opinions expressed by their owners. As such, I do not assume responsibility or liability for any third party material or opinions.

The publication of such third party materials does not constitute my guarantee of any information, instruction, opinion, products or services contained within the third party materials. The use of recommended third party materials does not guarantee any success and/or earnings related to you or your business. Publication of such third party materials is just a recommendation and an expression of my own opinion of that material. All trademarks and registered trademarks appearing in this guide are the property of their respective owners.

Cover image designed by Elisa Pulliam.

Dedication

*It is with great joy that I dedicate this
training manual to the 80 women who
brought the first M2B Mentoring Course to
life through their desire to impact
this world for the glory of God.*

Table of Contents

WEEK FIVE

WEEK SIX

Embrace Mentoring Training

So you feel called to be a mentor?

Perhaps you've even been asked by a young woman to mentor?

But do you know what to do next?

Do you feel a huge weight of hesitation about even trying to learn how to mentor effectively?

Well, we're pretty sure our six week mentoring training study using *Impact My Life: Biblical Mentoring Simplified*, along with the material in this study guide, will build your confidence and give you courage as you are inspired to draw nearer to Christ and move into positions of significant influence in a world desperately needing your impact.

The Journey Is Yours

Whether you are a twenty-something college gal, a stay-at-home mom of a tween or teen, involved in leading a youth group or women's ministry, this journey of mentoring training will speak to your heart and enable you to take steps toward personal growth. You have the opportunity to embark on this journey in one of three ways, all of which are compatible with the closed Facebook mentoring groups available through More to Be:

Instant Impact ~ approximately one hour a week
- Devote six weeks toward reading through this training manual.
- Read through the weekly recommended reading from *Impact My Life*.
- Answer the Take Time to Train questions found at the end of each chapter in *Impact My Life*.

High Impact ~ approximately two hours a week
- Devote six weeks toward reading through this training manual.
- Read through the weekly recommended reading from *Impact My Life*.
- Answer the Take Time to Train questions found at the end of each chapter in *Impact My Life*.
- Answer the Go Deep questions at the end of each chapter in this study guide.

Super Impact ~ approximately three hours a week
- Devote six weeks toward reading through this training manual.
- Read through the weekly recommended reading from *Impact My Life*.
- Answer the Take Time to Train questions found at the end of each chapter in *Impact My Life*.
- Answer the Go Deep questions located at the end of each chpater in this study guide.
- Complete the Weekly Worksheets located at the end of each chapter in this study guide.

{If you would like to download printable copies of the Go Deep questions and Weekly Worksheets, please go to http://www.moretobe.com/training/.}

You have the opportunity to personalize this training journey, based on what best fits your schedule and needs. Take some time to carefully consider the options, without putting pressure on yourself to do it all or do it perfectly. Any little bit of investment you put into this training will reap a great reward, because ultimately, it will draw you nearer to Christ and encourage you to become more intentional as you live out your faith.

I encourage you to pause right now and dedicate your study to the Lord, committing to Him your plan to learn and grow as a mentor. Ask the Lord for wisdom as to which level of study would be realistic for you, and ask him for discernment as you take a pulse on your expectations. I urge you to pray throughout this study. Pray for what you are to learn, who you are to connect with, and how you shall receive what is written.

Oh Lord, open my eyes to have me see you at work, receive what you would have me to learn, and respond with your heart to those I get to take this journey with online and in real life. Lord, enable me to focus each time I sit down to read and do the study. Father, give insight so that I may grow spiritually and emotionally through digging into this material. Rise up to the surface anything that is holding me back. Reveal to me your truth, that I may embrace it and live it out with those you've called me to impact. In Jesus' Name, Amen!

~ • ~

What is Biblical Mentoring?

It is time!

It is time to build on the principles found in *Impact My Life: Biblical Mentoring Simplified* by going deeper into the material and extracting key application points.

It is time to face our excuses while we simplify the mentoring process, making it doable for you — whether you are a twenty-something college gal, a stay at home mom raising her own children, a woman working with the youth group at church, a pastor's wife with a heart for women, a ministry leader, or simply a woman of any age seeking to impact others. So let's get going and discover how you can become an effective biblical mentor!

Oh That Mentor Word!

The word mentoring carries such a stigma, both positively and negatively. Those who have experienced the blessings of mentoring use the word with fondness and passion, understanding the purpose and seeing the tangible benefits. However, those who have never experienced healthy mentoring relationships tend to face the word with fear, hesitation, and sometimes a bit of bitterness or resentment.

I've been on both sides of the mentoring continuum. I've mentored others and have seen tremendous blessings in being mentored as well. Yet I also know that feeling of longing for a mentor and of growing resentful when I wasn't the one picked, so to speak. I'm sure my face turned three shades of red, embarrassed by my own intense jealousy, as I heard a woman I deeply respected publicly declare her mentoring role in the life of a woman nearly my age. I wanted that proclamation! And then, as I shared in Impact My Life, I remembered the truths

God impressed on my heart about the roles of mentors:

**The fact is that many women lack eyes to
see the opportunity to mentor and miss noticing
when they have been mentored by others.**

The truth is that I do have mentors, just not ones who have a platform from which they can announce their influence in my life. There are at least five women who I know, without a doubt, who exemplify what I describe as a biblical mentor in *Impact My Life* — women who follow Christ distinctly and from the overflow of that relationship, speak truth, life, and hope into my soul. Women who offer counsel based on the wisdom founded in the Word. Women who provide encouragement through their thoughtful actions and critical times of support. The world might simply call them friends, but I call them my biblical mentors because these relationships span the generations, occur outside of the routines of life seasons, and are rooted in our shared faith in Jesus Christ as Lord.

I wonder, when you think of biblical mentoring this way, what women fill this role in your life?

In *Impact My Life*, I share the iMentor Manifesto as a way of painting the picture of what mentoring looks like, both in being mentored and becoming a mentor. I think the reason so many women are intimidated by the idea of mentoring is because they've never seen it from this safe and simple perspective. I also believe that looking at the subtle but tangible ways we've been mentored by others equips us with a plan for how to mentor others. So if you haven't yet read Chapter Three, put aside some time this week to read it and answer the questions. This will be a critical step in developing your mentoring mind-set over the weeks to come.

So What is Biblical Mentoring and Why Is It Important?

Biblical mentoring, as I define it in *Impact My Life*, is a combination of discipleship as modeled by Christ and the principles of mentoring, used often in professional settings:

"Biblical mentoring is a combination of mentoring and discipleship. Jesus set the example for us in the way He came alongside the disciples, modeled his Father's instructions in action, answered their questions, responded to their needs and challenged them forward in their calling to glorify God. He was both their friend and their teacher. A mentor and a man who discipled others. He set a pattern for us to follow as we answer the call to go forth and make disciples.

...In a biblical mentoring relationship, the goal is to train the younger person or believer in every area of life,

10

not only through teaching but also by example, incorporating God and His word into every teachable spoken and silent moment." Impact My Life, p. 19 -20

When I think about why biblical mentoring has become so important to me, I realize it has much to do with the setting and culture in which we live. Our lives are busy. Our opportunities to deeply connect are few. Our focus is distracted. Our marriages are broken and families divided. Our mommas are working hard. Our emotional wounds are deep. Our guilt is paralyzing.

It is so easy to remain always in motion, never seeing the need before us to speak into the lives of others, especially the next generation. But this is not how God intended for us to live. Even 2000 years ago, women still met at a well and connected while drawing water to nourish their families. In doing so, they were nourished through the sharing of life together. Where does that happen today?

**With our cell phones beeping and carpools clamoring,
we don't connect unless we purpose ourselves to do so.**

And so we need to purpose ourselves toward connecting, applying the principles of biblical mentoring for the benefit of our relationships, with those who mentor us and with those we need to mentor. Our daughters and nieces, neighbors and friends, co-leaders and team members, all needing to know more of Christ, more of His hope, more of His perspective, and more about how to live out the Scriptures, practically, in a world that dismisses His truth for feeling and impulse.

**Biblical mentoring starts with us following Christ
distinctly, setting the example for the ones we love.**

By doing so, we're painting a 3D picture of what it looks like to live as a disciple of Christ. And then, when God provides that amazing moment to explain, reveal, communicate the Truth in Words, we seize it with confidence and share it with humble compassion. That's what biblical mentoring is all about.

What's Next?

Take time to read the **Introduction through Chapter 4** in *Impact My Life: Biblical Mentoring Simplified* and make the most of the following Go Deep questions and Weekly Worksheets.

~ • ~

What is Biblical Mentoring?

1. What is your definition of biblical mentoring? Feel free to record your preconceived notions of mentoring and how these perceptions might have changed due to reading *Impact My Life* or as a result of this first week's study content.

2. Can you think of any women in your life who have served as a mentor to you? If so, describe how they filled that role.

3. Can you think of anyone who have you have mentored, either intentionally or simply through doing life together? If so, describe who those people are and how the mentoring occurred?

4. What does it mean to you to follow Christ distinctly so that from the overflow you may mentor biblically?

5. Take time to read the following Scripture passages and record the ways these verse describe what it looks like to be a disciple of Christ.

John 1:35-51:

Romans 10:9-10:

Hebrews 4:12:

2 Timothy 3:16:

Romans 12:1-2:

Matthew 28:19:

John 14:26:

7. Rewrite Deuteronomy 6:5-10 as a prayer for your own life:

Deuteronomy 6:5-10 ESV

5 You shall love the Lord your God with all your heart and with all your soul and with all your might. 6 And these words that I command you today shall be on your heart. 7 You shall teach them diligently to your children, and shall talk of them when you sit in your house, and when you walk by the way, and when you lie down, and when you rise. 8 You shall bind them as a sign on your hand, and they shall be as frontlets between your eyes. 9 You shall write them on the doorposts of your house and on your gates.

iMentor Manifesto

One of the first steps toward becoming an intentional mentor is to look at how you are already mentoring and the ways in which you are being mentored. Take the time to use this worksheet to brainstorm and write out your own iMentor Manifesto. If you are stuck for ideas, you can refer to the examples provided in Chapter 3 in *Impact My Life: Biblical Mentoring Simplified*.

i mentor...

1.

2.

3.

4.

5.

i am mentored...

1.

2.

3.

4.

5.

How does this perspective change your feelings about mentoring in the future?

Facing Our Excuses

It is amazing to be part of a movement where God is raising up and calling forward women from around the world to step into significant mentoring roles. There are women of every age and every season seeking to be used by God in tangible ways, and they are learning they are qualified to mentor biblically when they follow Christ distinctly.

What a delight to see that college age gals embracing this training so they can better reach out to girls in their communities, pastors' wives are seeking ways to be more effective and intentional with women in their churches, moms are looking to love their daughters more purposefully, and more!

> *"Biblical mentoring is about doing real life together with real people. It is about being rooted in the word in order to apply it to every day life...It isn't so much about how you mentor, where you mentor, or who you mentor. You don't need a title or program! All you need is to feel the call personally and respond practically!" Impact My Life, p. 32*

We have a myriad of excuses that can so easily keep us from ever moving beyond theory and hold us back from the actual practice of mentoring. Wouldn't that be such a tragedy! So let's face our excuses head on and encourage one another to see God to working in us and through us to achieve his purposes through all our relationships for His glory.

What are the excuses that keep you from stepping into significant mentoring roles?

Are those excuses ones you've carried with you a long time?

Have these excuses been spoken to you or put upon you by others?

What would it look like to trump those excuses -- which are nothing more than lies -- with truths from Scripture?

In *Impact My Life*, we are challenged to face our excuses head on as we acknowledge that the enemy of God is out to steal, kill, and destroy each one of us, even though God's plans are that we may enjoy life to the fullest (John 10:10). The Lord desires to use us for His kingdom purposes, and to take pleasure in that co-laboring process.

Biblical mentoring is simply an intentional process by which we willingly surrender our insecurities, fears, and apprehensions to the Lord with a desire to see Him work in us and through us for His glory.

This step of surrender begins with looking at what is standing in our way: our excuses. I believe there are four primary excuses that knock at our insecurity door and cause us to waiver in our determination to become a mentor:

1. ...but I feel like a hypocrite
2. ...but I feel like I am too young
3. ...but I feel like I lack wisdom
4. ...but I feel like it is not my gifting

Which ones resonate with you?

Or do you battle another type of excuse?

The enemy's tactics are incredibly crafty and cunning, and almost always begin with a lie that spins into nothing short of the death of a dream, pursuit, purpose, or plan. Right now, our dream is to become women of influence, impacting the lives around us for the glory of God. We sense a need and want to respond. But that means we must be willing to do the hard work of battling the enemy of God with the truth!

Using Scriptures to Battle Excuses

Through looking at the Scriptures, as we do in *Impact My Life*, we can discern which core excuses have become deeply embedded in our lives, and search the Scriptures for an applicable truth. For example, the issue of feeling like a hypocrite often paralyzes women from speaking into the lives of others. Often, a woman is too afraid to give advice or offer direction, especially if she has made a mistake in that particular area in the past. But as we look at Scripture, we can find the confidence through embracing the truth. For example:

Example One

> **Belief or Core Lie:** I can't mentor, because I messed up by doing [fill in the blank].

> **Truth**: Romans 3:23 ESV "...for all have sinned and fall short of the glory of God..."

> **Applying of the Truth to the Core Lie:** I have made "this" mistake. Yes, I have sinned. But the Scripture tells me all have sinned. If I believe that only people who haven't sinned could mentor, than no one could ever mentor. Therefore, the truth is that my sin does not prevent me from being qualified to mentor. The truth is that God redeems my sin through faith in Jesus Christ and in Him, I can confidently go forth to mentor others.

Example Two

> **Belief or Core Lie**: I can't mentor because I've already set such a bad example by doing [fill in the blank].

> **Truth**: 1 Corinthians 11:1 ESV, "Be imitators of me, as I am of Christ."

> **Applying of the Truth to the Core Lie:** If I believe my mistakes prohibit me from mentoring, then my focus is on myself. But instead, my focus should be on imitating Christ and encouraging those I mentor to do the same. Therefore, I can mentor, even if I've made mistakes, because I am not encouraging others to follow me, but to follow my example as I follow Christ. And where I fail to follow Christ, I can also model confession and repentance.

By applying the Scriptures to our excuses -- again and again as they arise in different shapes and forms -- we can move into the positions of influence God is leading us toward.

Using Coaching Principles to Mentor

In addition to applying the truth to the core lies that keep you from mentoring, you can also implement a few basic life coaching principles. Life coaching is an interesting and emerging field -- which is foreign to many people -- so let me explain the role of a life coach and the benefit of using coaching techniques in your mentoring.

Phases of Life Coaching

A trained life coach is qualified to come along side a person to help them in four basic phases or areas of life:

Awareness:
Figuring out what is going on in life, what is working, not working, and areas that need focus.

Vision:
Determining where you want to go, what you want to accomplish, including ideal as well as practical goals.

Obstacles:
Identifying what is standing in the way of your vision becoming reality.

Strategies:
Pinpointing solutions to overcome the obstacles in you life and how to move toward your vision.

Life coaching is not counseling.
Counseling deals with foundational issues that rest under the surface of life, like an archaeologist who digs to uncover what happened in the past and the impact it has on today. A counselor is also trained to respond to emotional, spiritual, and even physical issues, where as a coach is sensitive to those matters, but is not trained to dig in and bring about healing.

Life coaching is accountability and encouragement.
A life coach functions more like an architect, who enables the building process. If there are issues along the way, a coach may be able to help their client in an isolated instances, but healing from the past is not the overall purpose the relationship. Instead, the goal is to help process what is happening present day in order to identify practical solutions.

Life coaching uses questions to find solutions.
What is unique about the coaching relationships is that the coach primarily uses questions to help the client determine for herself (and through the working of the Holy Spirit) appropriate solutions to her current issues. As a Christian life coach, the foundational belief is that Jesus is the one who has the answers the client is looking for, and as a coach the desire is to seek the Lord for the right questions to ask so that the client will draw nearer to Him.

Life coaching is not mentoring.
As we've been studying, a mentor is someone who will directly teach and speak humbly but

boldly into a mentoree's life. A mentor may directly tell a person what they should do and how they should go about it, whereas a coach will typically not give a directive and if they do offer an instruction, they would first ask permission.

A mentor can benefit from using coaching techniques.
A mentor can certainly utilize life coaching principles, through asking questions and seeking permission before sharing instructions, opinions, or personal stories. Through approaching mentoring (and even parenting)with a coaching mind-set focused on asking questions, the burden to have all the answers is be lifted making the overall experience much more rewarding.

**The greatest gift a mentor can give is the
companionship of life, not all the right answers.**

When someone comes to you with a problem to solve or for advice on a challenging situation, abiding by coaching principles will enable you to step into the role of companion, rather than feeling like a savior who needs to have all the answers. For example, a mentor who responds with a coaching mind-set will be able to:

- Listen to their mentoree's questions and story carefully.
- Shape her responses to their needs with questions.
- Restate what they hear their mentoree saying, both in her heart and words.
- Encourage a strength in their mentoree, which is hopefully related to the situation.
- Ask for permission before they share their own story enabling the focus to remain on the mentoree and situation at hand!

There is nothing like discovering that you don't have to have all the answers! By applying life coaching principles in my own mentoring relationships (and especially in my parenting), I've witnessed how the door to serve on my knees -- seeking the Lord for His wisdom -- has positioned me to be of greater help to those I deeply care for and long to impact.

Through asking questions before offering answers, you really will be able to offer practical help and encouragement.

What's Next?

Take time to read **Chapters 5 through 9** in *Impact My Life: Biblical Mentoring Simplified* and make the most of the following Go Deep questions and Weekly Worksheets.

~ • ~

Facing Your Excuses

1. What are the excuses that keep you from stepping into significant mentoring roles?

2. Are those excuses ones you've carried with you a long time?

3. Have those excuses been spoken to you or put upon you by others?

4. What would it look like to trump those excuses with truths from Scripture?

5. This week, we talked about how the enemy sets about to steal, kill, and destroy, but that God desires for us to have life to the fullest. Take time to write out John 10:10 in at least three different translations, which you can find at Biblegateway.com.

John 10:10:

Use John 10:10 as a framework for speaking with the Lord. Name those things you can pinpoint as the enemy's work and ask the Lord for his redemptive power to be displayed gloriously. Speak honestly with the Lord about your desires for the full life He promises, and for vision to see clearly, from His perspective, what that means.

You may also want to look up and rewrite the additional verses:

Isaiah 61:1-4:

Romans 8:28-29:

1 Corinthians 1:3-4:

Genesis 50:20:

2 Corinthians 3:3:

Naming Your Excuses

As we discussed in week two of this study, we need to face our excuses in order to move forward in our mentoring goals. Use this worksheet to record your excuses and to write down the truths found in the Word that pertain to those excuses. Use may want to use Biblegateway.com or a concordance in your Bible to find verses related to your struggles. Also devote time to prayer, seeking the Lord for answers and being willing to sit quietly to allow Him to speak to your heart.

I highly recommend thinking of this as a living document without a deadline. Facing our excuses is an ongoing process, so treat it with much grace, as you await on a revelation from God meant exactly for you. If you find yourself stuck, may I suggest brainstorming with a Christian friend who might be able to provide another perspective? You might also be in a place where there are no excuses plaguing you. Praise the Lord! Put this sheet aside and enjoy a time of being with God, praising Him for this gift!

excuse...   **truth...**

1.

2.

3.

4.

5.

A Guide for Responding to Questions

As a mentor, you will inevitably face times in which you'll be presented with a challenging situation or a request for advice. Sometimes a mentoree will ask you a simple question or want you to give specific directions. At times, you may feel you have the answer, while at other times you may feel totally clueless. In either scenario, follow these life coaching principles indicated below so that you'll position yourself to respond with the heart of God, while placing your mentoree before the Lord as you seek Him together for the answers.

1. **Listen to their question and story carefully!** You don't want to make assumptions or jump to conclusions, so pay attention to what they are saying, and sometimes, what they are not saying!

2. **Shape your response with questions!** Don't tell them the answer! The Lord has the answer for them, and your role is to help them seek Him. Through asking questions, you get the other person thinking from a new angle or perspective. This also helps you to join them in their journey, giving them confidence to grow and pursue the Lord personally. As they respond to your questions, they will discover the answer, or you will recognize more questions you can ask.

3. **Restate what you hear!** Again, you need to make sure you're on the same page. Restating what you hear also helps them to know you are listening and engaged.

4. **Encourage a strength!** Look for a character strength you see in them that would build their confidence to press on. This also helps guard you from jumping into fix-it mode as you focus on their abilities and God-given strengths.

5. **Ask for permission to share your story!** This isn't about you, so keep the focus on them. If you have a story relevant to their experience, ask for permission before you share it. This guards you from becoming a run-away-story-train, derailing from their growth and putting the focus on you. Asking permission to share your story puts the mentoree in a teachable position, since they have to agree to listen to you.

While this process may feel awkward, you will be amazed at how it effectively it works. When a person feels as though they came up with an answer to their problem or situation, they are much more likely to embrace the solution.

WEEK THREE

Well It's Not About Me!

In *Impact My Life*, I discuss in how we all have excuses that prevent us from mentoring and from becoming the women God intended. This tactic of the enemy is intentional, for he knows that when he undermines our confidence, he stops our effectiveness and impact. In our effort to fight off Satan's influence, last week we looked at the top four excuses most women experience in their journey of becoming a mentor:

1. ...but I feel like a hypocrite.
2. ...but I feel like I am too young.
3. ...but I feel like I lack wisdom.
4. ...but I feel like it is not my gifting.

But.

But these aren't the only excuses. Right? There are more excuses, like...

...but my family is such a mess.
...but I struggle with knowing what to say.
...but my life is in chaos and I can't seem to make headway.

But!

Which one is yours?

There will always be a but. One that is uniquely yours. Yet that doesn't mean you have to put the brakes on stepping out as a mentor.

Unless...

Yes, there are seasons of trials and transitions, which we can't and shouldn't begin significant mentoring relationships. There may also be times in which we need to pull back from our commitments, especially when we notice that what is flowing out of our mouths reflects a heart issue that needs serious attention.

Your Mouth Can Show You What You Really Need to Do!

God has given us a beautiful way to determine whether we should be in active mentoring relationships. Matthew 12:34 instructs, "For whatever is in your heart determines what you say." If we put ourselves in a position of intentionally mentoring others, we need to be keenly aware of our emotional and spiritual health.

Are we speaking words of bitterness, anger, frustration? Are we jaded about a particular situation, experience, person (even groups of people, such as men, women, political leaders, Christian leaders, ethnic groups) due to a wound or inherited bias?

When our words reveal our hurting hearts, it is a clear indicator that we need to focus on personal healing.

Occasionally, we can embark on this healing journey with the Lord and continue to maintain our mentoring relationships. However, there are other situations in which the wounds run deep and lies have written over God's truth, requiring that we seek out help to move forward and heal.

One of the best things we can do for ourselves and those we love is take a step of faith into solid Christian counseling. Yes, I've had to do this multiple times! Christian counseling was key in God's work of showing me the effects of my hardened and bitter heart and open my soul up to His transforming work (Ezekiel 36:26). It is only a myth that getting help proves weak faith. Counseling is a tool God uses to heal broken and wounded souls. It isn't a life-time commitment, but will have a life-time benefit.

Remember, it is about what He is doing in you and through you!

As you work through your excuses and take time to inventory your heart, do so with this truth in mind: It is God who equips you for the relationships He ordains for you.

God qualifies you through your relationship with His
Son.

Through your faith in Jesus Christ as Lord, you are completely qualified to go forth as a disciple of Christ, free to share His love and hope and truth. His transforming power is at work in your life. No matter how little you see. No matter how short of a time you've lived for Him. No matter how many mistakes you've made (and will continue to make.)

God's grace is all over you, girlfriend, qualifying you
to impact others with Biblical truth the minute
He calls you His own.

And it is ultimately about them...

Have you ever noticed our tendency to focus too much on ourselves? That's what happens when we lock in on our excuses and forget that God is the one working in us and through us. One of the ways we can move out of self focus is by using the Three Story Technique. This technique will also reshape how you approach all your relationships.

Three Story Technique

Story 1: What is your story?

What do you believe about yourself? About your life? About God? What is your faith like? How are you growing deeper spiritually? What is your next step in your journey of spiritual maturity? What is it about your life circumstances and relationships -- past and present -- and your hopes for the future, that make you unique. In other words, know who you are and embrace the significance about the story God is writing of your life.

Story 2: What is their story?

What does it look like to take an interest in their life, especially in tangible ways that allow you to get to know them? As you spend time together, seek to learn more about who they are and what they believe. Ask questions to discover details about their life circumstances and relationships -- past and present -- as well as their hopes for the future. Don't go on a mission to hunt down problems and fix their issues. Rather, receive them as they are, and pray for the work of God to be accomplished in their life.

Story 3: What is His story?

The most important story to discover is the one about Jesus Christ. In this relationship, you have the opportunity to share the Gospel message, power of the cross, and promise of eternity. Become a student of the Word and be comfortable sharing the story of God in conversation. Seize opportunities to share the Gospel message and biblical principles throughout the maturing of your relationship. It is His story that matters most of all.

Becoming a biblical mentor requires us to step outside of ourselves, our insecurities, and our preconceived notions in order to notice the needs of those around us and recognize the way we are perfectly suited to serve. As members within the body of Christ, we each have a particular role to fill, unique to our gifts, talents, and experiences. It is part of our story and HIStory!

**In our completely imperfect, messy but beautiful lives,
we can become women of godly impact.**

But first, we have to stop evaluating whether we measure up and identify the people we can, in faith, reach out to, trusting God to write the whole story for His glory. Because it is really about Him and THEM!

What's Next?

Take time to read **Chapters 10 through 12** in *Impact My Life: Biblical Mentoring Simplified* and make the most of the following Go Deep questions and Weekly Worksheets.

~ • ~

Well It's Not About Me

1. What is your main "but" excuse? And what truth from Scripture trumps that excuse?

2. What were your thoughts about the Three Story Technique? How do you think it will work for you? Do you need to get to know your story better? Do you need to understand God's story better? If so, what should your next step be toward growth?

3. In this week's study, we looked at the biblical principle found in Matthew 12:34, which instructs, "For whatever is in your heart determines what you say." Based on this truth, how would you describe what is going on in your heart? Are there wounds festering and breeding bitterness? Is there unforgiveness and guilt or shame? Take the time to journal about the state of your heart below.   If you don't have a pulse on your spiritual heartbeat, please spend time in prayer and reflection this week. Write down what you hear yourself saying, and seek the Lord in learning what it all means. Please don't feel shy about seeking professoinal help or the counsel of a pastor, either.

4. Look up Matthew 12:34 in multiple translations. Write down at least three different versions, and then turn Matthew 12:34 into a Scripture prayer.

Three Story Technique

In this week's study, we looked again at the excuses that keep us from impacting lives with biblical mentoring, but we didn't stay there. Instead, we moved on into the truth, recognizing that mentoring is really about what God is doing in us and through us for the benefit of those around us.

I also introduced the concept of the "Three Story Technique," which is a mindset that enables you to think intentionally about your relationships without getting overwhelmed by yourself. In order to begin to "feel out" how this works, you can use this worksheet to spend time in prayer and reflection, working out the three story technique on paper.

For Story One
Look at the questions provided and begin the process of answering them in a simple sentence without all the details. You can go back to this step and add more detail in time.

For Story Two
You may not know for whom these questions will apply, so use this time to pray and seek the Lord about whom you should mentor. If you have children, you might want to complete these questions about them and ask the Lord to give you insight as to how to serve them as a mentor.

For Story Three
Begin the process of articulating how you would like to communicate the Gospel message. This might be a good time to write down key verses or find websites online that can become your "go-to" resources when introducing the Gospel to someone who is not yet a Christian.

Story One: You

1. What do you believe about yourself?

2. Your life?

3. About God?

4. What is your faith like?

5. How are you growing deeper spiritually?

6. What is the next step you believe you should take in order to further mature as a believer?

7. What is it about your life circumstances and relationships -- past and present -- and your hopes for the future, that make you unique?

8. In other words, know who you are and what is significant about the story God is writing of your life.

Story Two: Them

{you may like to reproduce this page to complete for each person you are mentoring}

1. What does it look like to take an interest in their life, especially in tangible ways that allow you to get to know them?

2. As you spend time together, what have you learned about who they are and what they believe?

3. What details about their life circumstances and relationships -- past and present -- as well as their hopes for the future, are important for you to know?

4. Are you on a mission to hunt down problems and fix their issues, or are you receiving them as they are and praying for the work of God to be accomplished in their life?

Story Three: Him

1. The most important story to discover is the one about Jesus Christ. Who is Jesus?

2. How would you explain the Gospel message?

3. How would you describe the power of the cross?

4. How do you express the promise of eternity?

5. Are you a student of the Word? If not, what steps should you take to become one?

6. Are you comfortable sharing the story of Christ in conversation? If not, is there someone you can practice with?

Remember, it is His story that matters most of all.

Mentoring in Action

Mentoring Is Like...

In order for us to answer the call to mentor, we have to grow in our understanding of what mentoring really is. So far in this study, and in our reading of *Impact My Life*, we are discovering truths to enable us to paint a bigger picture about mentoring.

We've determined that in order to mentor biblically we must first follow Christ distinctly. We've also looked at the many excuses that wreck our mentoring confidence and cause us to pull back rather than step in. Now it is time to step out, as we look for who we can mentor and how to do that effectively.

A Baton Pass...

In *Impact My Life*, I used the analogy of a baton pass in a relay race as a way to describe the dynamics of mentoring relationships. Essentially, if you want to run your leg well, you need to consider your agility as a runner as well as your skill in handling the baton pass. You have to train for both aspects of the race. Likewise, as a mentor you are both running your leg of race -- your journey of life and faith -- while also seeking to pass the baton to the next generation. In other words, you can be in a position of receiving mentoring from others while also actively mentoring the next generation or those spiritually less mature.

So who do you think you might run this race with?

- mother to daughter
- aunt to niece

- college senior to a college freshman
- thirty-something mom with kids to a twenty-something newly married
- a situation totally unique to your life

Mentoring does not need to be defined by your season of life.

It can be very organic, as in the relationship formed between a mom and her children's baby-sitter, or more traditional, as in a youth leader to the girls in her youth group. The circumstances that apply to the relationship are not as important as the eternal investment.

Do You Hear the Call?

To be honest, I never really decided to become a mentor. I simply saw a need in the lives of the girls around me, and boldly stepped into their lives. Because I live at a boarding (and day) high school, it was natural for me to connect with the teenage girls crawling all over the place. They reminded me of myself, and so I would connect with them in the ways I had wished older woman would have reached out to me.

As King Solomon writes in Ecclesiastes, there is nothing new under the sun. Girls have issues. The same ones that we, the adults in their lives, faced at their age and still struggle with today. So, one by one, for many years, I'd invite a girl for tea with a desire to encourage her. I must admit, I really hoped to fixed all her issues so that her life could be better than mine was at her age.

But you know what I learned?

I can't fix her. Or her. Or her.

**But I can respond with the love and hope of Christ,
because He is the fixer of all things this
side of heaven until eternity.**

Eventually, my one-on-one times became group times, with the formation of ETC (which stands for Evening Tea & Chat, which is the name of the mentoring group I host for teenagers. You can find details for starting your own ETC group for tweens, teens, or twenty-somethings at moretobe.com/etc.). That's why I began writing the curriculum-without-the-binding (i.e., Topics & Truth Downloads available at moretobe.com), which eventually inspired the creation of More to Be. From the overflow of what was happening in real life, God was burning a fire in my heart to equip others to step into mentoring relationships. It was only as this all came together, that I realized I was not only a mentor to teens, but I was also becoming a mentor of mentors.

Dimensions of Mentoring

Mentoring is unexpected.

It can certainly be planned for and structured, like ETC.

But mentoring doesn't always need a title, date, or time.

**See, mentoring often happens when you choose to invest
in the lives around you without a title,
method, or program.**

That's what I was doing with our weekly baby-sitters. I cared about Brannon and Natalie simply because God gave me a heart for them. I wanted to know what was going on in their lives and share mine with them, too. As I write about in *Impact My Life*, my husband and I would come home from our date nights with enough time left so that I could chat with the girls. Over the years, our conversations were "influence bookmarks" in their lives. They were listening to what I said -- and didn't say -- taking notes about how I lived my life and determining if I would be one of their trusted adults.

Our time was setting a foundation for the future, fixing me into a part of their story in a way that only God could ordain.

He also fixed them into a part of mine as they invested in my own children. They listened, prayed, and loved on all our children, impacting their lives in a priceless way.

Do you see the baton pass?

As I loved on these teens, they loved on my family. But there is part of this pass I haven't even mentioned. See, my mother modeled this for me, and she didn't even know it. She too brought a teenager into our family as a weekly baby-sitter. Rose Ann loved on us, and my mother loved on her. Well beyond our baby-sitting years, my mom maintained a relationship with Rose Ann through occasional phone calls and letters, even after we moved away. I am sure my mom was simply being who my mom is -- a kind woman who cares deeply for others. She didn't realize that her example would impact me by setting a natural example in how to connect beyond the family walls.

What's the Pattern?

As I share my story, I can already hear your excuses. But I don't have money for a baby-sitter! But I don't even know any teenagers to ask to baby-sit! But I don't have kids!

Okay, so step back and look at the pattern, not the details.

This pattern of one woman to another, is the same one that jumps out of the Scriptures. As I watched the Nativity Story again this past Christmas season, it was stunning to me how Elizabeth filled a Titus 2 mentoring role in Mary's life. God's purposes pre-ordained that relationship to give Him the glory. Couldn't that be true for all mentoring relationships? Shouldn't we see the willingness of Mary to seek out Elizabeth, and Elizabeth's willingness to serve Mary, as an example for how we are to live in Titus 2 mentoring relationships (Luke 1:39-42)?

Do you see the pattern I see?

- They knew each other but were not a part of each other's daily lives until the need presented itself.
- Mary knew she could turn to Elizabeth in her time of need.
- Elizabeth responded with joy in meeting Mary's need.
- Their time together was meant for a season.

As we look at this pattern, I want you to ask yourself: In which relationship can I become more intentional so as to take advantage of opportunities to invest organically into another's life?

Who can you come alongside and encourage?

If you have children, are there older kids from church or your neighborhood who you can bring alongside your family? How can you embark on mentoring without it costing money? Did you ever think that maybe a young person isn't interested as much in the mighty dollar as you think? Could it be that they would simply love hanging out with you, or your kids? We have so many misconceptions about each other. Let's put aside our excuses and get mentoring, regardless of our age, season, or financial situation.

You are on your way toward mentoring authentically and purposefully. To help you take the next step and think outside the box, dig into the homework opportunities and begin to apply the principles in *Impact My Life*.

What's Next?

Take time to read **Chapters 13 through 16** in *Impact My Life: Biblical Mentoring Simplified* and make the most of the following Go Deep questions and Weekly Worksheets.

~ • ~

Mentoring in Action

1. As you consider mentoring in action and the example of the baton pass, what relationships in your life currently fit this description? Write down how they are playing out. If there are none, consider the reasons and what it would require for this to change.

2. Are there women and/or girls in your life currently who you think you ought to "run this mentoring relay race" with in an intentional way? If so, what is the next step you can take? Take a few minutes to pray about your ideas and discern whether these thoughts are from the Lord.

3. We looked at the pattern set in the relationship between Mary and Elizabeth. Pause to read the Luke 1:39-42 and write down what you discover. Also spend time in prayer, asking God to speak to you specifically about this type of relationship between an older woman and a younger woman, as you consider what it means to you personally?

4. Who in your life can you invest into in an organic way? Who can you come alongside and encourage?

5. If you have children, are there older kids from church or your neighborhood that you can bring alongside your family?

6. How can you embark on mentoring without it costing money?

7. Look up Titus 2:3-5 in multiple translations. Write down at least 3 different versions, and then write down the many different ways women are called to engage with and impact the next generation.

Map Out Your Mentoring

This week in our study, we began looking at mentoring in action with a focus on relationships. By looking at the example of running a relay race with a baton pass, we considered what it would look like to be in both organic and purposeful mentoring relationships.

1 Corinthians 9:24
Do you not know that in a race all the runners run,
but only one receives the prize?
So run that you may obtain it.

Considering ourselves as runners in a race is consistent with Scripture. We are urged in 1 Corinthians to put on the mind-set of a runner, whose goal is on the prize. For us, the prize comes when we've lived this life to glorify God as we await to meet Him in eternity. With that perspective in mind, use this worksheet to help you brainstorm about the relay-race-like mentoring relationships in your life. With yourself in the center, draw lines to connect yourself to those people in your list of "influencers." These may be your mentors, whether the relationship is intentional or organic. Then draw lines to connect yourself to those people on the right in your "impacting" list, which represents those you feel called to mentor.

If you feel like there is nothing to write down, use this space to dream and pray about what you long for and would like God to accomplish in your life in terms of the relationships you have the opportunity to experience, be refreshed by, and impact.

Influencers   **Impacting**

ME

Nine Steps of Mentoring

In the last chapter, we looked closely at the pattern of mentoring relationships, establishing that they are like a baton pass in a relay race, where one generation is reaching out and enabling the next generation to press on while equipping them to finish well. In this chapter, it is time to take that theory and put it into practice.

Putting the Pattern to Work

What exactly does it look like to run that mentoring race in real life with real people?

As we've talked about throughout the study, mentoring can happen in multiple ways, such as:

Formal (Planned) Mentoring

- older woman to a younger woman with a set meeting time
- serving as a youth group leader
- leading a women's ministry team
- teaching Sunday school
- working with a group of youth
- leading a mentoring group

Informal (Organic) Mentoring

- mother to daughter
- older sister to a younger sister
- aunt to a niece

• working with youth in a particular setting and using the opportunities that arise to mentor

Regardless of the relationship or setting, there are some basic principles to consider in pursuing intentional mentoring that will help cultivate healthy, appropriate relationships while maintaining boundaries.

Nine Steps of Mentoring

In *Impact My Life*, I use the word "mentoring" as our navigation tool. With each letter standing for a different aspect of mentoring, we have nine simple steps to consider as we mentor:

1. Meeting
2. Encouraging
3. Noticing
4. Teaching
5. Offering
6. Responding
7. Inspiring
8. Navigating
9. Growing

Honestly, these nine steps are significant in every relationship, even though they may not be applied consciously. As we embrace a mentoring mind-set, however, we want to use these nine steps as a guide by which we can prayerfully and purposefully consider how we impact the next generation and those younger in their faith walk. These nine steps also provide a great framework for setting up a formal mentoring relationship, which in the long run will aid in minimizing conflict, resentment, and disappointment.

Real Life, Real Relationships

So how do the nine steps of mentoring actually play out in real life? Impact My Life offers step-by-step instructions for each of the nine steps of mentoring, considering details like what is reasonable for setting up a meeting time and how to go about responding to what you see and hear in a mentoree's life.

Rather than giving you the play-by-play here, I want to paint a picture for you, so that you can see how these nine steps play out in different relationships and situations through sharing my personal experiences. But please don't get hung up on my examples! Let them inspire you to seek God for yours! The Lord is carefully and purposefully creating your unique mentoring opportunities, so resist the urge to give labels to relationships and confine experiences to a box. Rather, embrace what the Lord has for you today.

With Children and/or Siblings

I consider myself a mentor to my children first and foremost. If I'm not engaging them in a way that will leave a lasting impact, who will? So I use the nine steps of mentoring as an evaluation tool. Through time in prayer as well as through discussion with my husband, the nine steps serve as a checklist for making sure I eternally invest in my children.

For example, I might ask myself, "When was the last time I intentionally listened to Leah? Did I encourage her when she came to me last night? Was I responding to her heart or her needs this morning? How am I helping her navigate and grow through these challenges? What was the last eternal and practical thing I taught her?"

As a result of asking these questions of myself as I seek the Lord (sometimes in the moment), I am challenged by the Holy Spirit working within me to make the necessary changes in order to be more intentional.

With Individuals

The nine mentoring steps serve as a guide for my individual mentoring relationships. For example, in my relationship with a twenty-something married who approached me for mentoring, our meeting time happens over the phone about once a month and through email once a week. The goal is to encourage her to grow in her spiritual maturity, ministry, work, and marriage, so I ask key questions about those areas to learn about what is going on in her life and look for opportunities to teach, inspire, and help her navigate the course ahead.

With a few of my college gals, we connect by email every few weeks and in person when they are home for a cup of tea or a meal with my family. Because our relationship was established over years together, these mentoring conversations are like check ups. Again, I ask a lot of questions and look for "kick-in-the-pants" moments to help them navigate through their situations.

With the teens I mentor individually, I find in this season there are many five minute conversations and a once a month catch up time. I use the nine steps to remind myself to notice their needs and pray for them often, even though the teaching time is minimal.

If I am approached by a someone seeking one-on-one intentional mentoring, I start off by talking with her about what she is looking for and then present her with these nine steps as a way for us to decide together the best ways to approach our relationship.

With Groups

For me, I love the way mentoring can take place in a group setting. ETC and Mugs & Mornings is a perfect example of a group mentoring situation, where a number of girls come to my home for teaching and encouragement. The date, time, and teaching material (Topic & Truth Downloads) is set in place before they even walk in the door.

When it comes to noticing and responding, I carefully watch each girl, from the moment they arrive. I'm looking at body language and eye contact to discern what is going on in their hearts. I seek the Lord throughout this time, asking Him to whisper to my heart about their needs, while actively looking for ways to inspire each of them and enable them to navigate life once they leave my home.

This kind of group mentoring is exhilarating for me, especially when I am blessed with mentoring partners. These sister-mentors may sit quietly during our gathering, but I know they are praying hard. I love to see each one engage according to their own personality and witness the valuable role they play in the one-on-one follow up time.

We are working together, as the body of Christ, dancing through the nine steps of mentoring according to the Master's beautiful choreography.

Mentoring will happen whether we choose to be intentional about it through using a group format or casually coming alongside a mentoree. Simply doing real life together requires real relationships, right? But imagine if those relationships took on a whole new perspective! Imagine if you paused monthly to pray about your impact and seek God for His work in the lives of those you already love? Imagine if you put into place even half of the ideas mentioned in *Impact My Life* for living with healthy and wise boundaries! Imagine!

What's Next?

Take time to read **Chapters 17 through 21** in *Impact My Life: Biblical Mentoring Simplified* and make the most of the following Go Deep questions and Weekly Worksheets.

~ • ~

Nine Steps of Mentoring

1. How do you feeling about running the mentoring race in real life, with real people? Are you intimidated? Exhilarated? Afraid? Eager?

2. Looking at the nine steps of mentoring, which areas come naturally to you? Which ones do you consider weaknesses? For those areas, are there people or resources you could use to help you grow? For a great list of books and links, visit More to Be and look through the Resources tab.

    - Meeting

    - Encouraging

    - Noticing

    - Teaching

    - Offering

    - Responding

    - Inspiring

    - Navigating

    - Growing

3. Now take some time to reflect on the people that fit into the three different types of mentoring relationships. Write down their names and note the ways in which you are already mentoring them according to the nine different steps.

- Mentoring Children and/or Siblings:

- Mentoring Individuals:

- Mentoring Groups:

4. As you consider those relationships you noted above in light of the nine mentoring steps, consider the ways in which you could be more intentional in your mentoring. Journal here about those possibilities and pray for the Lord's will in those relationships.

5. Now it is time to dig into Romans 12, which offers an excellent set of life application instructions for all our relationships, and an provides guidance as to our individual part within the body of Christ. Read through this passage two times and look up three different versions. Then turn this passage into a prayer for yourself. To go even deeper, turn it into a prayer for the mentorees God has put on your heart.

Romans 12:1-21 ESV

A Living Sacrifice

I appeal to you therefore, brothers, by the mercies of God, to present your bodies as a living sacrifice, holy and acceptable to God, which is your spiritual worship. 2 Do not be conformed to this world, but be transformed by the renewal of your mind, that by testing you may discern what is the will of God, what is good and acceptable and perfect.

Gifts of Grace

3 For by the grace given to me I say to everyone among you not to think of himself more highly than he ought to think, but to think with sober judgment, each according to the measure of faith that God has assigned. 4 For as in one body we have many members, and the members do not all have the same function, 5 so we, though many, are one body in Christ, and individually members one of another. 6 Having gifts that differ according to the grace given to us, let us use them: if prophecy, in proportion to our faith; 7 if service, in our serving; the one who teaches, in his teaching; 8 the one who exhorts, in his exhortation; the one who contributes, in generosity; the one who leads, with zeal; the one who does acts of mercy, with cheerfulness.

Marks of the True Christian

9 Let love be genuine. Abhor what is evil; hold fast to what is good. 10 Love one another with brotherly affection. Outdo one another in showing honor. 11 Do not be slothful in zeal, be fervent in spirit, serve the Lord. 12 Rejoice in hope, be patient in tribulation, be constant in prayer. 13 Contribute to the needs of the saints and seek to show hospitality.

14 Bless those who persecute you; bless and do not curse them. 15 Rejoice with those who rejoice, weep with those who weep. 16 Live in harmony with one another. Do not be haughty, but associate with the lowly. Never be wise in your own sight. 17 Repay no one evil for evil, but give thought to do what is honorable in the sight of all. 18 If possible, so far as it depends on you, live peaceably with all. 19 Beloved, never avenge yourselves, but leave it to the wrath of God, for it is written, "Vengeance is mine, I will repay, says the Lord." 20 To the contrary, "if your enemy is hungry, feed him; if he is thirsty, give him something to drink; for by so doing you will heap burning coals on his head." 21 Do not be overcome by evil, but overcome evil with good.

Nine Steps of Mentoring Guide & Checklist

As you seek to mentor intentionally, one of the greatest things you can do for those you desire to impact is to bring them before the Lord in prayer and walk humbly in the way you engage in your relationship.

On the following page is a tool that is designed to enable you to build this sort of accountability into your mentoring experience. Mark down a time on your calendar to meet with the Lord about those you are in relationship with and desire to mentor. Then print out multiple copies of the second page of this worksheet and fill one out for each person the Lord has brought into your life to mentor.

You might want to set aside more than one time a month to do this sort of accountability check, such as setting aside one day for your children or family members (older siblings, you can become a great mentor to your younger siblings), another for individuals outside your family, and another for groups. To keep track of all your mentorees, jot down their names below and tick off the month in which you do your check up.

	Name	**Date of Check In**
1.		
2.		
3.		
4.		
5.		
6.		

Mentoring Accountability Checklist

Date: **Name:**

As you look at each of these nine steps, jot down anything that comes to mind in regards to how you need to participate in the relationship, what you need to bring to the Lord in prayer, and any matters that concern you and require follow-up or conversation with your mentoree.

1. Meeting

2. Encouraging

3. Noticing

4. Teaching

5. Offering

6. Responding

7. Inspiring

8. Navigating

9. Growing

Launch with Impact!

From the very beginning of this study, I've emphasized that it is our faith in Jesus Christ as Lord and our place in the family of God that enables us to live a life of impact. Our ability to become a godly influence on those around us as we invest in:

- our daughters
- a neighbor down the block
- a group of girls from youth group
- the women on our ministry team
- our younger siblings
- our younger friends living down the hall from us in the dorm

Our mentoring begins with how we are living daily before the King.

Oh friends, living out our faith is no small task!

Becoming a woman who devotes time to meeting with the Lord, studying the Word, yielding her heart in prayer, and growing in her faith through the iron-sharpening-iron relationships within the body of Christ is nothing short of a challenge. Our culture doesn't encourage this type of devotion and discipline. We have practical needs demanding our attention every day. Who's going to fold the laundry? Pay the bills? Get the family where they have to go? Who's going to do our homework? Serve at church on Sunday morning? Finish our last task at work before rushing home?

It often feels like the buck stops right here, with you and me, doesn't it?

How can we put off any of those necessary things in order to make time for our relationship with God?

Hmm...

Doesn't that question sound a little bit like the enemy's whisper telling us it just isn't possible?

Battling the Lies

Are we being duped by lies from the pit of hell, tempting us to believe that we simply don't have the time to invest in our relationship with the Lord? That if we even try, we risk not getting everything else done and further risk letting down our family and friends?

My Confession

Oh my, I must confess. I have struggled to put off the tyranny of the urgent to devote time to God for many days of my Christian walk. Even this morning, as I write this post, I was tempted to skip my quiet time. Only by the grace of God pushing on my conscience, did I flip the computer lid down and open my prayer journal.

> *Heavenly Father, I give you this day. Please order it according to your purposes and show me your work that I might join you in it...*

I penned a few thoughts pressing on my heart.

> *Amen.*

And off I hurried to get back to my work. Until I felt another nudge.

> *Read your Bible, too. Don't skip this step.*

A deep sigh. I opened up to the passage I've been studying in 1 John using the *Overflow Method* (available at More to Be). I know I need to do this, yet I resist. Why?

Because sometimes, I just want to knock down my to do list more than I want to spend time reading my Bible.

Sometimes, I don't want to do the Christian thing and be all disciplined and devoted.

True to my personality, I waffle from one extreme to the other. I've been "Super Bible Woman" plenty of times, abandoning the dishes in the sink, while I've lunged into my Bible study homework, not caring who walked into the house. But those times seem to mark the season when

70

I was a desperate momma in need of Jesus.

Time in the Word was like air for me to breathe.

Beyond the desperate years, there have been before dawn seasons of sitting quietly with the Lord and soaking in the presence of the Holy Spirit.

But that is not my normal life.

Oh no. I've spent as many, if not more days, battling a desire to withdraw from God, sometimes out of disappointment, and other times because I want to do something more exciting, like, um, surf the internet. Watch a TV show. Sleep a little later. Shop a little longer. Conquer my idea-slinging list like super woman.

I suppose that if we looked closely at the pattern of my devotion to the Lord, it would clearly coincide with the rhythms of my life and the trials upon my world. When life falls apart...ahem... cancer, injuries, depression, rejection, loneliness, adulteries, divorce, division...I run to God. At first. But when I feel like He doesn't answer, I run away. Until I come to my senses and dive back into His arms. Sometimes.

Mentors Can't Have a Temperamental Faith

My faith is as temperamental as my personality, but by God's grace, He's convicted me that this weakness needs serious attention. My faith ought not to be based on feelings. Neither should yours.

> **To grow into that woman who mentors biblically,
> we need to invest the time into our relationship
> with the Lord daily.**

There, I said it.

If we are going to follow Christ distinctly, we need to do more than know of Christ, we need to know Christ personally.

And we get to know Christ by spending time in the Word, allowing the Holy Spirit time to teach and guide us in all truth (John 15:26).

Spiritual Insurance Policy

So what can we do to counter the cultural pull away from devoting time to the Lord? How can we develop the discipline we need in order to discover the fullness of Christ through His word? We need to figure out who we are, with all honesty about our life, have a loosely held plan for our quiet time, and embrace grace so that we can pursue the discipline of spending time with God daily.

1. KNOW YOU

God made you unique, with a particular learning style and personality. This certainly affects your relationship with God and how you learn His word. By identifying your personality and learning style, you can choose a Bible study method and quiet time routine that best suits you. For example, I have a life coaching client that discovered she feels closest to God in nature, so she started taking prayer walks as a way to spend time with the Lord. Suddenly, her spiritual life felt vibrant again, simply by adding this habit into her routine.

2. ACCEPT LIFE

Take the time to look at your life and evaluate your schedule (download free time evaluation resources from elisapulliam.com). Decide on a realistic approach for spending your time with the Lord and in the Word. Maybe this isn't the season in which you should do an inductive Bible study, but you can make time to read a chapter of the Bible a day on your smart phone.

3. MAKE A PLAN

Make a short term plan for how you are going to devote time to being with the Lord and in His word each week. Decide on a time, place, and what you'll do for your quiet time routine. *The Overflow Study Method* could be a great way for you to get started.

4. EMBRACE GRACE

Every day will bring new challenges and unexpected situations. It is great to have a plan in place, but embrace God's grace for you when you fall short and stumble. Don't give up, but face each new day with the new mercies God offers you.

Essentially, I like to think of time in the word and meeting with the Lord daily like a spiritual insurance policy. It won't prevent the trial that might come your way, but it will certainly draw you closer to the Lord and equip you to face the trial when it comes (Lamentations 3:22-23).

Time to Launch

Over the course of the last six weeks, we've looked closely at what it means to mentor biblically. We've identified our excuses and trumped them with the truth! We've looked at the power of story to connect lives together in the context of the Gospel. We've considered the pattern of mentoring set before us in Scripture and opened our eyes to the possibility of mentoring relationships all around us. And we've looked at the nine steps of mentoring as a guide for how, when, and where we should put on a mentoring mind-set. Finally, today, we've focused on getting our own faith journey in working order.

**So now, friends, it is time to launch forward,
guided by the principle that when we follow Christ distinctly,
we're powerfully equipped and qualified to mentor biblically.**

As I share throughout *Impact My Life*, as well as in this study, the process of mentoring can be organic or planned. It can be spontaneous, simply by putting on a mentoring mind-set as you engage with those in your family and church, or purposeful, as you step into leadership positions with a ministry team, youth group, or by beginning your own ETC or Mugs & Morning mentoring group (find all the information you need at moretobe.com). The logistics of how, when, and where you mentor will depend upon how the Lord is calling you to minister through the relationships with those He brings into your life.

The most important thing you can do as you wait upon God to reveal your next mentoring move, is to turn and face the cross, pressing into your relationship with Him (Philippians 3:13-15). The cross is where the life of a biblical mentor must always begin and remain (Hebrews 12:2). When you are bowed at the foot of the cross, you will hear the call and know that you are equipped. It is there you will receive the fullness of the One that you long to give away.

Ephesians 3:14-21 MSG

My response is to get down on my knees before the Father, this magnificent Father who parcels out all heaven and earth. I ask him to strengthen you by his Spirit—not a brute strength but a glorious inner strength—that Christ will live in you as you open the door and invite him in. And I ask him that with both feet planted firmly on love, you'll be able to take in with all followers of Jesus the extravagant dimensions of Christ's love. Reach out and experience the breadth! Test its length! Plumb the depths! Rise to the heights! Live full lives, full in the fullness of God.

God can do anything, you know—far more than you could ever imagine or guess or request in your wildest dreams! He does it not by pushing us around but by working within us, his Spirit deeply and gently within us.

What's Next?

Take time to read **Chapters 22 through 24** in *Impact My Life: Biblical Mentoring Simplified* and make the most of the following Go Deep questions and Weekly Worksheets.

~ • ~

Launch with Impact

1. Are you tempted to put off your time with the Lord in order to get the necessary things of life done? If so, what are those necessary things?

2. When you choose those necessary things instead of spending time with the Lord first, what is the thought that plays through your mind? How does this thought line up with biblical truth?

3. How do you most enjoy spending time with the Lord? Be creative and think outside of the box! Write down every idea:

4. What way do you most enjoy praying? Is there a method, place, or style that works best with your personality? How can you incorporate this into your life weekly?

5. When it comes to digging into the Word, what method, style, or routine works best for you? Is this currently part of your daily/weekly life? If not, what would it take to make it happen?

6. Are you connected with the body of Christ, in a local church, small group, or Bible study? If not, what nudge do you need to move in that direction?

7. What would it take for you to be motivated to put the necessary things off for 20 minutes a day in order to spend it with the Lord in Scripture and study?

8. Take the time to read Philippians 3:13-16 in three different versions. What sticks out to you? How could this passage relate to your personal faith walk? Rewrite the passage as a personal prayer.

   Philippians 3:3-16 MSG

   I'm not saying that I have this all together, that I have it made. But I am well on my way, reaching out for Christ, who has so wondrously reached out for me. Friends, don't get me wrong: By no means do I count myself an expert in all of this, but I've got my eye on the goal, where God is beckoning us onward—to Jesus. I'm off and running, and I'm not turning back. So let's keep focused on that goal, those of us who want everything God has for us. If any of you have something else in mind, something less than total commitment, God will clear your blurred vision—you'll see it yet! Now that we're on the right track, let's stay on it.

A Different Kind of Insurance

As we learned in this week's lesson, it is critical for you to meet with the Lord on a regular basis, devoting time to prayer and the studying of Scripture, so that you are prepared to face life's ups and downs, especially as a mentor. When trials come your way, you want to be better prepared with a strongly established faith, an understanding of who God is, and the richness of Scripture dwelling within your mind for the Holy Spirit to draw upon.

Developing the discipline of spending time with the Lord and in the Scriptures is going to look different for every person, so rather than trying to model your habits after someone else, dig into discovering what would work best for you by knowing who you are, the reality of your time, and the best way you study Scripture. Most importantly, may I encourage you to remember to embrace grace, as you are a work in progress.

1. Know Yourself

There are many ways to go about identifying who you are and how God has naturally wired you. The following web-based services are a good starting point for self-discovery. Keep in mind that I can not guarantee their results or what they stand for theologically, so please use discernment if you choose to use these services.

Identify your personality:

- http://www.41q.com/
- http://www.123test.com/disc-personality-test/

Discover your spiritual gifts:

- http://www.churchgrowth.org/cgi-cg/gifts.cgi?intro=1
- http://www.spiritualgiftstest.com/
- http://www.ministrymatters.com/spiritualgifts/#axzz2Jak71tRH

Pinpoint your learning style:

- http://www.howtolearn.com/learning-styles-quiz

- http://www.edutopia.org/multiple-intelligences-learning-styles-quiz

2. Accept Your Life

In order to make time to be with the Lord and in the Word you need to figure out what is realistic. Use these free tools to help you evaluate your time and sketch out a plan for going forward.

Download a time evaluation and life mapping worksheet:

- http://www.elisapulliam.com/2013/01/21/steps-toward-living-in-balance/

Identify your options for study and prayer

- Overflow Method - http://www.elisapulliam.com/2012/12/31/from-overwhelmed-to-overflowing-bible-study-and-time-management-method/
- Immersed Method - http://www.moretobe.com/immersed/
- List of Helpful Websites - http://www.moretobe.com/websites-for-mentors/
- Lists of Books - http://www.moretobe.com/books-and-studies-for-mentors/

3. Make a Plan

Based on your evaluation and research, now put a plan in place.

- What is a realistic amount of time for you to spend with the Lord each day?

- What time of day will you meet with the Lord?

- What method will you use for studying Scripture and praying?

- How long will this plan take you to finish? Or what is a goal for the number of weeks you'll keep at it?

- What reward can you give to yourself when you meet your goal?

4. Embrace Grace

When you set forth a plan to devote time to spend with the Lord, the enemy is going to crouch nearby ready to pounce on you. To prepare yourself, establish an "embrace grace" mind-set that you can "go to" when you feel defeated.

- What three verses can you cling to when you feel discouraged?

- What will be your action/response plan if you miss a day? Or more?

- What do you consider reasonable or acceptable excuses (illness, travel, sleepless night with kids) for which you can miss your appointment with God?

As as life coach, I am available to help you put this all in place and hold you accountable. For more information, please feel free to email me at elisa@elisapulliam.com or visit http://www.elisapulliam.com/life-coaching/services/.

Acknowledgements

It is only fitting after putting together a study guide such as this to thank all those who made it possible. But the question is where do I begin? Let me start at the top. Jesus. My Savior makes any word that comes from my hands possible. Thank you Lord for using a woman like me to equip your daughters to live a life of impact.

Second in line is the man who has been Christ with skin on to me. Thank you, Stephen, for more than two decades of showing me His love and cheering me on with nearly every idea that comes through my crazy mind. And of course, my children, follow in my husband's footsteps, blessing me beyond measure. You rise each day with love for me. I close each day thanking God for the blessing of each of you. Words can not ever express my love for each of you.

Apart from my family, this study is truly the result of the *More to Be* Team, which includes over thirty women sacrificing their time, their hearts, and their words for the sake of impacting teens, influencing moms, and inspiring mentors. Their praying and supporting hours made room for these words to grow and bloom. Thank you, sisters. I couldn't do this without you. I have to give a special thanks to Josie, Suz, and Sarah for their attentive editing and proof-reading eye! What a gift you are to this not-so-detail-oriented gal!

I also want to thank my precious sisters-in-Christ who are a part of my Brew1024 Mastermind group. They offered their support, encouragement, and feedback through the process of putting together this study guide.

And lastly, it is a joy to thank the 80 women who participated in the first M2B Mentoring Training Course. They cheered on this project, validated its need, and urged me on to the finish with their steadfast support. Thank you, MITS, for your faith steps in this journey together. I am humbled to serve you and am blessed by your partnership in the Gospel. May you go forth and impact this world for God's glory!

About the Author

Elisa Pulliam, who prefers to be called Lisa, is a lifelong mentor, ministry leader, speaker and life coach, passionate about encouraging and equipping this generation of women to impact the next generation with relevant Truth.

After more than a decade of mothering and over fifteen years of mentoring teen girls coinciding with leading women's ministries, Elisa is in tune with the struggles of teens, twenty-somethings and today's women. Having lived a life apart from God, marked by a legacy of dysfunction and a long season of rebellion, Elisa understands the power of the Cross. When she met Jesus as her Lord and Savior during her junior year in college, her life radically changed, and her life calling soon emerged.

Elisa's deepest desire is to facilitate life transformation in others by offering practical, easily accessible, and biblically sound resources to touch the heart, mind and soul. She shares her insights, teaching materials, and mentoring resources at *More to Be*, and offers life coaching through elisapulliam.com. You can also find her contributing monthly at Mothers of Daughters. com, and The Better Mom.com. Although her schedule is full, she is refueled by hosting regular ETC gatherings for teen girls, speaking at women's events as well as for groups of teenagers. Her goal is to make the most of their time through capturing biblical truths through storytelling, transparently sharing her personal experiences, and tossing in a good bit of humor as she unravels life lessons.

Elisa's counts it pure joy to be Stephen's wife, who is not only her best friend but has been Christ-with-skin-on to her for seventeen years of marriage. She also considers it a privilege to train up her four children (ages 8 through 14), and admits that they have taught her the most about love, affection and total forgiveness.

Ephesians 3:7
By God's grace and mighty power, I have been given the privilege of serving him
by spreading this Good News.

About More to Be

More to Be is dedicated to engaging the next generation through equipping moms of tweens and teens with biblically relevant resources and encouraging women to step into significant mentoring roles.

Through providing simple, easily accessible online resources, *More to Be* is committed to speaking to the hearts of tween, teen and twenty-something girls, while also influencing today's moms to be the vessels of Truth in their daughter's lives and to see Christian women to step out in faith in answering the call to mentor the next generation of young women.

- Online mentoring training and studies courses encourage women to follow Christ distinctly so that they may mentor biblically. Built on principles captured by Elisa Pulliam in her book, *"Impact My Life: Biblical Mentoring Simplified,"* (available on Amazon), the courses incorporate life coaching concepts with discipleship principles to equip all women to mentor.

- ETC. Mentoring and Mugs & Mornings Mentoring, presents a unique mentoring concept providing a format and collection of resources designed to equip women to lead mentoring groups in their homes and community.

- Topics & Truth FREE downloadable lessons (really curriculum without the binding) and Dig Deep Guides, provide a quick but thorough look at relevant topics steeped in biblical truth.

- Life Coaching is available for especially for mentors and moms looking to develop leadership and life skills as they discover how to use their God-given gifts and talents in a variety of settings.

- The Blog is a daily landing place, full of encouragement, relevant Truth, informational articles, and interesting links for today's teens, twenty-somethings, mentors, and women.

At the heart of *More to Be* is a vision to see women (young and old) become more bright, more beautiful, more like Jesus as a personally relevant God enters their lives (2 Corinthians 3:16-18 MSG) through mentoring relationships and resources grounded in biblical truth. This is what it means to experience life transformed -- a life where there is more to be as we become more like Him and impact the world around us.

If you have any questions about *More to Be*, please email more@moretobe.com or visit www. moretobe.com.

2 Corinthians 3: MSG
...when God is personally present, a living Spirit....Nothing between us
and God, our faces shining with the brightness of his face. And so we are
transfigured much like the Messiah, our lives gradually becoming brighter and
more beautiful as God enters our lives and we become like him.

Have you been impacted?

I'd love to hear from you!

elisa@moretobe.com

elisapulliam.com

Spread the Word

We'd love for you to share about More to Be and
our M2B Mentoring Training Course with others!

moretobe.com

facebook.com/moretobe

twitter.com/moretobe

pinterest.com/elisapulliam

39532764R00053

Made in the USA
Lexington, KY
27 February 2015